EVOLVE

WORKBOOK

Mari Vargo

3B

T0306685

CAMBRIDGE
UNIVERSITY PRESS

CAMBRIDGE
UNIVERSITY PRESS

University Printing House, Cambridge CB2 8BS, United Kingdom

One Liberty Plaza, 20th Floor, New York, NY 10006, USA

477 Williamstown Road, Port Melbourne, VIC 3207, Australia

314–321, 3rd Floor, Plot 3, Splendor Forum, Jasola District Centre, New Delhi – 110025, India

103 Penang Road, #05-06/07, Visioncrest Commercial, Singapore 238467

Cambridge University Press is part of the University of Cambridge.

It furthers the University's mission by disseminating knowledge in the pursuit of education, learning and research at the highest international levels of excellence.

www.cambridge.org
Information on this title: www.cambridge.org/9781108411936

First published 2019

20 19 18 17 16 15 14 13 12 11 10 9 8 7 6 5 4 3

Printed in Poland by Opolgraf

A catalogue record for this publication is available from the British Library

ISBN 978-1-108-40527-0 Student's Book
ISBN 978-1-108-40507-2 Student's Book A
ISBN 978-1-108-40920-9 Student's Book B
ISBN 978-1-108-40528-7 Student's Book with Practice Extra
ISBN 978-1-108-40508-9 Student's Book with Practice Extra A
ISBN 978-1-108-40921-6 Student's Book with Practice Extra B
ISBN 978-1-108-40900-1 Workbook with Audio
ISBN 978-1-108-40872-1 Workbook with Audio A
ISBN 978-1-108-41193-6 Workbook with Audio B
ISBN 978-1-108-40517-1 Teacher's Edition with Test Generator
ISBN 978-1-108-41068-7 Presentation Plus
ISBN 978-1-108-41203-2 Class Audio CDs
ISBN 978-1-108-40793-9 Video Resource Book with DVD
ISBN 978-1-108-41447-0 Full Contact with DVD
ISBN 978-1-108-41154-7 Full Contact A with DVD
ISBN 978-1-108-41415-9 Full Contact B with DVD

Additional resources for this publication at www.cambridge.org/evolve

CONTENTS

UNIT 7 ENTERTAIN US

7.1 A 50-YEAR PLAYLIST

1 VOCABULARY: Music

A **Find 9 more vocabulary words in the word search.**

classical country ~~EDM~~ folk heavy metal hip-hop jazz pop reggae rock

C	D	L	A	B	H	R	T	I	M	W	X	P	D	E	R	Y
A	C	O	U	N	T	R	Y	N	S	N	H	E	K	M	F	O
C	E	Y	V	D	F	E	U	S	Q	K	F	W	C	P	O	P
E	X	E	E	K	W	C	D	E	L	V	R	U	O	S	L	E
B	H	E	C	R	O	S	Q	A	H	E	V	Y	B	E	K	P
S	I	L	J	R	E	G	G	A	E	S	Y	V	B	U	W	X
H	P	C	U	R	F	K	L	W	A	B	E	D	M	R	P	E
D	H	L	W	J	X	U	S	F	V	K	E	H	D	W	C	J
Q	O	U	J	A	Z	Z	E	C	Y	H	O	L	L	W	E	B
M	P	S	A	L	O	M	S	W	M	A	J	I	E	C	R	L
K	E	D	V	Y	E	W	H	I	E	C	Y	G	N	R	E	I
T	R	T	S	I	V	A	R	E	T	E	C	H	N	O	D	A
S	T	A	S	K	W	L	O	E	A	S	B	E	Y	C	M	Q
W	C	L	A	S	S	I	C	A	L	S	X	Y	N	K	B	I
X	T	R	O	N	W	C	I	S	U	D	D	U	M	T	H	Y

2 GRAMMAR: *used to*

A **Complete each sentence with the subject and verb in parentheses ( ). Add the correct form of *used to*.**

1 A Where *did you use to buy* your music? (you / buy)

B ________ it in music stores. (I / get)

2 A ________ to rock music when he was a teenager? (he / listen)

B No, ________ rock music. (he / not like)

3 A What kind of music ________ when she was young? (your mother / like)

B ________ heavy metal. (she / love) ________ classical music, but she likes it now. (she / not listen to)

4 A ________ to a lot of concerts before you were born? (your parents / go)

B No, concerts were expensive. But ________ a lot of jazz CDs and listen to them together. (they / buy)

5 A "I Want You Back" by *NSYNC ________ my favorite song when I was in high school. (be)

B ________ that pop song! (I / hate) ________ it on the radio constantly! (they / play)

B Circle the correct words to complete the sentences.

1 I *used to go / went* to a dance class three times a week, but I hated the music we had to dance to!
2 I *used to come / came* home at 6:00 a.m. after the New Year's Eve dance party in 2016.
3 My aunt and uncle *didn't use to sing / didn't sing* "Happy Birthday" to my cousin when she turned three. They completely forgot!
4 My best friend *used to make / made* the best playlists before we studied for all of our big tests.

3 GRAMMAR AND VOCABULARY

A **Complete each sentence with the correct form of *used to*, the verb in parentheses ( ), and a word or phrase in the box.**

~~classical~~ EDM heavy metal jazz pop hip-hop reggae

1 Susan used to listen to classical music a lot because she played piano and violin. (listen to)
2 Jack ______________, but now he thinks it's too loud and the singers sound like they're screaming. (enjoy)
3 Eric ______________ music because it was so fast and he couldn't understand the words. (not like)
4 Sam ______________, but after his vacation to Jamaica, he started to listen to it all the time. His favorite singer is Bob Marley. (not listen to)
5 Linda's grandfather ______________ in the 1930s. He was the saxophone player in a band. (play)
6 I ______________ music, but I don't like it anymore. I deleted all the Katy Perry and Britney Spears songs from my music app. (like)
7 My friends ______________, but then I took them to some dance clubs, and now they love it! (not care about)

B **Correct the mistake in each sentence.**

1 My friends and I use to go to concerts a lot. My friends and I used to go to concerts a lot.
2 Did you used to listen to pop music? ______________
3 I wasn't use to like reggae. ______________
4 Where did you usually use to listen to music? ______________
5 Do you use to have a favorite band? ______________
6 What kind of music do your favorite band used to play? ______________

C **Answer the questions in exercise 3B and add details. For the statements, rewrite them as questions.**

1 Did you and your friends use to go to concerts a lot?
2 ______________
3 ______________
4 ______________
5 ______________
6 ______________

7.2 THE BEST ENTERTAINMENT

1 VOCABULARY: TV shows and movies

A **Match the words with the correct TV or movie genre.**

1 information, real, learn	____	a	comedy
2 prize, games, host	____	b	documentary
3 frightening, suspense, surprise ending	____	c	game show
4 entertain, laugh, jokes	____	d	science fiction
5 imaginary, future, technology	____	e	thriller

B **Complete the sentences with the correct words or phrases in the box.**

comedy	horror	game show	~~documentary~~
musicals	reality show	talk show	

1 We watched a ___documentary___ about climate change in my biology class.
2 My friend won $5,000 on a ________________ . She answered all the questions correctly.
3 Do you watch this ________________ ? It always has good guests, and the host is so funny.
4 I can't watch ________________ movies when I'm home alone. I get too scared.
5 I like to watch ________________ shows when I come home from work. They make me laugh.
6 I don't ever want to be on a ________________ . My life is private.
7 I like ________________ if the songs are good.

C **Complete the sentences with the correct words or phrases in the box.**

animated movies	soap opera	dramas	romantic comedies	science fiction	thrillers

1 *Star Wars* is the first ________________ movie that I saw.
2 That actor is in a lot of ________________ . He usually plays a police officer or a spy.
3 I like to make digital drawings. I want to make ________________ when I'm finished with school.
4 Sometimes I don't like to watch ________________ because they're too serious for me.
5 Gina likes to watch her favorite ________________ every day at 2:00. The characters are always fighting or falling in love.
6 Some people think only women like ________________ , but I know a lot of men who like funny movies about people falling in love.

2 GRAMMAR: Comparisons with *(not) as … as*

A **Unscramble the words to make sentences with *not as … as*.**

1 as / not / The second / good / first movie / as / the / movie is / .

____

2 like the / you / season / season / as / second / much / the first / Did / as / ?

____

3 movie is / good / The / as / not / the book / as / .

____

4 shows have / dramas / as / as / Reality / excitement / much / .

____

3 GRAMMAR AND VOCABULARY

A **Read the situations. Then write sentences with the words in parentheses ( ) and *(not) as … as*.**

1 She always likes learning things. She sometimes likes scary movies.
(not like / horror movies / documentaries)
She doesn't like horror movies as much as documentaries.

2 It's kind of fun to watch people talk. It's a lot of fun to watch people answer questions for money.
(talk shows / not fun / game shows)

____

3 I like watching serious movies. I also like watching movies about space or the future.
(like / dramas / science fiction movies)

____

4 Movies about crime and spies are really exciting. Scary movies are also really exciting.
(thrillers / exciting / horror movies)

____

B **Write sentences with *(not) as … as* that are true for you. Use the words in parentheses ( ) from exercise 3A. Add details.**

1 *I don't like documentaries as much as horror movies. Horror movies are much more exciting!*

2 ______________________________

3 ______________________________

4 ______________________________

7.3 A NEW BAND

1 FUNCTIONAL LANGUAGE: Refusing invitations and responding to refusals

A **Put the conversations in order.**

Conversation 1

B I'm sorry. Unfortunately, I have plans on Sunday. ____
B I'd love to, but I have to work on Saturday. ____
A I understand. Let me know if your plans change. ____
A Do you want to go out to dinner on Saturday night? ____
A Oh, that's too bad. How about lunch on Sunday? ____

Conversation 2

B I think I want to stay home on Friday. But thanks for asking. ____
B I have to finish my paper right now. Maybe after that. ____
A Yeah. I need to buy some new shoes. ____
A I understand. Let me know if you change your mind. ____
B Right now? ____
A Do you want to go shopping with me? ____
A OK. Oh, are you free on Friday? Jack and I are going to the movies. ____

2 REAL-WORLD STRATEGY: Softening comments

A **Soften each comment with *kind of* or *sort of*.**

1 Unfortunately, I'm busy tonight.
____

2 I'd love to, but I'm tired.
____

3 I'm sorry, but I think romantic comedies are silly.
____

4 No thanks. I think talk shows are boring.
____

5 Unfortunately, it's late.
____

3 FUNCTIONAL LANGUAGE AND REAL-WORLD STRATEGY

A **Write conversations using the ideas in the pictures. One speaker makes an invitation and the other speaker refuses the invitation. Soften the refusals.**

Conversation 1

A *Do you want to see a romantic comedy with me tonight?*

B ______________________________

A ______________________________

Conversation 2

A ______________________________

B ______________________________

A ______________________________

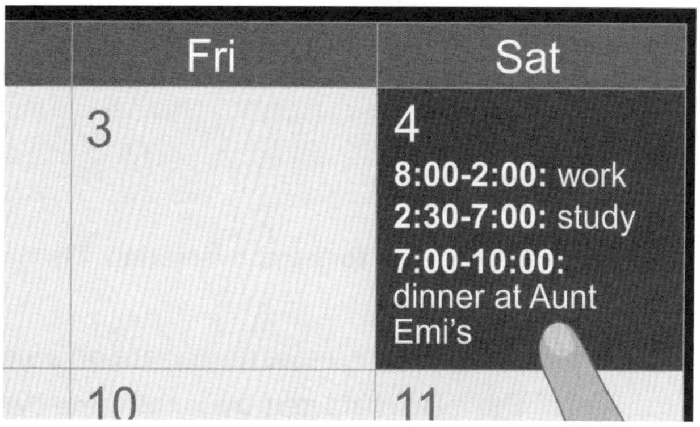

Conversation 3

A ______________________________

B ______________________________

A ______________________________

7.4 NOT JUST FOR KIDS

1 READING

A **READ FOR DETAIL** **Read the article and complete the sentences with information from the text.**

Why Do We Binge-Watch TV Shows?

How do you watch shows? Do you watch one episode a week? One a day? Or do you sometimes watch entire seasons in a weekend? If you like watching episode after episode of a series, you're not alone. Binge-watching has become more and more popular in the past few years. But why?

STRESS RELIEF When we binge-watch, we escape from our real lives for a few hours. While we're watching, we don't think about our problems or responsibilities. That can help us relieve stress.

HAPPINESS According to experts, when we binge-watch, our brains produce *dopamine* – a chemical that makes us feel happy. As soon as one episode is over, we start the next one because we want to keep feeling good.

CARING Psychologists say that our brains can experience things we watch on TV almost the same way that they experience real events. So we often become attached to stories and characters and really care about what happens to them. Because our brains aren't always good at separating episodes on TV from real life events, we have a strong desire to keep watching to find out what happens next.

Based on this information, it seems like binge-watching is a good thing – at least in the short term. However, over time, experts say that it can cause depression. When we finish binge-watching a series, we can feel a sense of loss. We can also feel sad because our brains stop producing dopamine.

1 When we binge-watch, we can forget about our ________ and ________.
2 Binge-watching helps us get rid of ________.
3 Binge-watching makes us feel ________.
4 When we see something happen in a TV show, our brains think we're experiencing it ________.
5 We can get really attached to the ________ and ________ in a show.

B **Do you think it's a good idea to binge-watch shows? Why or why not?**

____

____

2 LISTENING

A 7.01 **Listen to the conversation. Then read the statements and check (✓) *True*, *False*, or *Not given*.**

	True	False	Not given
1 Ken's favorite movie takes place on a weekday.	☐	☐	☐
2 The main characters are in the same class.	☐	☐	☐
3 The story takes place in the school cafeteria.	☐	☐	☐
4 It's a musical.	☐	☐	☐
5 The movie shows us that people are alike.	☐	☐	☐

3 WRITING

A Write a conversation in which you recommend a movie you have seen to a friend. Include the kind of movie it is, a short description, and at least three reasons why you like it.

A ______________________________

B ______________________________

A ______________________________

B ______________________________

A ______________________________

B ______________________________

A ______________________________

B ______________________________

A ______________________________

B ______________________________

CHECK AND REVIEW

Read the statements. Can you do these things?

UNIT 7	Mark the boxes. ☑ I can do it. ? I am not sure. **I can …**	If you are not sure, go back to these pages in the Student's Book.
VOCABULARY	☐ **talk about different types of music.** ☐ **talk about TV shows and movies.**	page 66 page 68
GRAMMAR	☐ **use *used to*.** ☐ **make comparisons with *(not) as … as*.**	page 67 page 69
FUNCTIONAL LANGUAGE	☐ **refuse invitations.** ☐ **respond to refusals.** ☐ **soften comments.**	page 70 page 70 page 71
SKILLS	☐ **write a movie review.** ☐ **organize ideas.**	page 73 page 73

UNIT 8 GETTING THERE

8.1 SAYING AND DOING

1 VOCABULARY: Describing experiences

A **Match each word with its definition.**

1 achievement *d*		a a chance to do something
2 challenge ____		b a difficult task
3 change ____		c a planned task
4 opportunity ____		d a particular thing that you have done successfully
5 project ____		e something different from what you were doing before

B **Match more words with their definitions.**

1 chore ____	a an attempt that ends in a good result
2 process ____	b something that you do to make money
3 job ____	c an ordinary task that you do regularly, like cleaning
4 success ____	d the steps involved in doing something

2 GRAMMAR: Present perfect continuous

A **Complete each question with a word or phrase in the box. Then answer the questions so they are true for you.**

Has	Have	I	someone in your class
What has	~~Where have~~	your mom and dad	

1 **A** *Where have* you been working?
B *I've been working in the library, but on Saturdays I work in a café.*

2 **A** ____________ 've been working a lot. What about you?
B ____________

3 **A** Have ____________ been reading a lot of books lately?
B ____________

4 **A** ____________ your best friend been doing this week?
B ____________

5 **A** Has ____________ been learning how to cook?
B ____________

6 **A** ____________ you been taking music lessons recently?
B ____________

7 **A** ____________ anyone been calling or texting you every day?
B ____________

B **Complete the sentences with the subjects and the present perfect continuous forms of the verbs in parentheses ( ).**

1 What ___have you been doing___ these past few days? (you / do)
2 ______ a Spanish class. (I / take)
3 ______ how to paint. (she / learn)
4 ______ out a lot? (you and your friends / go)
5 ______ a lot this summer. (we / travel)
6 ______ all afternoon. (he / call)

3 GRAMMAR AND VOCABULARY

A **Complete the sentences with the present perfect continuous form of the verbs in parentheses ( ) and a word in the box.**

achievement	~~chores~~	job	process	project

1 He ___has been doing___ ___chores___ at home all morning – vacuuming, doing laundry, washing dishes. (do)
2 I ______ on a new ______ at the office. It's almost finished. (work)
3 I ______ about the ______ of creating a handmade book. There are a lot of steps. (learn)
4 I ______ for a new ______. I'm not happy at work. (look)
5 She ______ hard for this ______. She just graduated from college. (work)

B **Answer the questions. Give examples.**

1 What opportunities have you been taking advantage of lately?

______
______
______

2 What have you been having the most success at lately: school, home, or work? Explain.

______
______
______
______
______

3 What kinds of challenges have you been dealing with in your academic or professional life lately?

______
______
______
______
______

8.2 STARTED, BUT NOT FINISHED

1 VOCABULARY: Describing progress

A **Write each phrase in the correct place in the chart.**

concentrating on	didn't have a chance	doing my best	getting nowhere
~~having problems~~	having trouble	making good progress	taking it easy

Fast or focused progress	Slow or no progress
	having problems

B **Complete the conversation with the correct forms of the verbs in the box.**

have	save	spend	waste

A You've been [1] ____________ a lot of time working on your new website lately, haven't you?
B Yeah, I learned how to code, so I can [2] ____________ time and work more quickly.
A That's great. Do you think you'll [3] ____________ time to help me with my website?
B Well, not today. My computer crashed! I've [4] ____________ a lot of time trying to fix it. I can't figure it out.

2 GRAMMAR: Present perfect vs. present perfect continuous

A **Circle the correct verb form to complete each sentence.**

1. I've *looked* / *been looking* for a new job for the past month.
2. I've *had* / *been having* three job interviews so far.
3. I've *worked* / *been working* part-time during my job search.
4. She's *gone* / *been going* to the supermarket five times this week.
5. She's *tried* / *been trying* new recipes since she started her cooking classes.
6. She's *taken* / *been taking* cooking classes for a few months.

B **Find and correct mistakes in <u>four</u> of the sentences. If a sentence is correct, write *correct*.**

1 I've read three books this month.

correct

2 She been spending a lot of time with her family lately.

3 We've clean the whole house.

4 I've been worked all day.

5 He have gone to Hong Kong twice.

6 We've been traveling for a week.

3 GRAMMAR AND VOCABULARY

A **Complete each sentence with the present perfect or present perfect continuous form of the verb in parentheses ( ) and a word or phrase in the box.**

a chance	a lot of time	it easy	my best	nowhere

1 I decided that I need a break, so I ______________ lately. (take)

2 I ______________, but I still can't work as quickly as you can. I'll keep trying. (do)

3 Oh no! This is the wrong paint! I ______________. Now I have to paint all the walls again. (waste)

4 I ______________ on this project after three days of work, so I'm moving onto a different one. (get)

5 I ______________ to read this book yet, but I'm going to start reading it tonight. (not / have)

B **Answer the questions.**

1 When you're having trouble at work or school, who do you talk to about it? Why?

2 Do you know a way to save a lot of time at work, at home, or on the way to work? Describe one way.

3 Where do you go when you have to concentrate on work or schoolwork and you don't want anyone to bother you?

8.3 HOW HAVE YOU BEEN?

1 FUNCTIONAL LANGUAGE: Talking to someone you haven't seen in a while

A **Put the conversations in order.**

Conversation 1

B I know. I haven't seen you since last summer! ____
B Good, thanks. What have you been up to? ____
A Hi, Mateo! It's been a long time. ____
B The same as usual. ____
A So, how have you been? ____
A Not much. I've just been going to school. What's going on with you? ____

Conversation 2

A The same as usual. She works all the time. What have you been up to? ____
A I've been really busy. I have to travel a lot for my job. Oh, hey, I saw Dasha last month. ____
B Not much. I've been looking for a new job. ____
A It's great to see you again, Melinda! It's been a long time. ____
B I know. What have you been doing? ____
B Really? What's going on with her? ____

2 REAL-WORLD STRATEGY: Using *that would be* to comment on something

A **Write a comment about each statement using *that would be* and the best adjective in the box.**

awful	exciting	fun	great	interesting

1 **A** I heard that Alan might lose his job.
B ______________________. He really needs that job.

2 **A** Do you want to have lunch at Luigi's Italian restaurant tomorrow?
B ______________________. I love Luigi's.

3 **A** Sook and I are going ice-skating tomorrow. Do you want to join us?
B ______________________. Sook always makes me laugh.

4 **A** I'm thinking about going on a trip around the world.
B ______________________. You should do it!

5 **A** Do you want to come with me to a lecture about space travel?
B ______________________. I read a lot of books about the future of space travel.

3 FUNCTIONAL LANGUAGE AND REAL-WORLD STRATEGY

A **Read the situations. Complete the sentences with phrases from the box.**

have you been	haven't seen you	it's been
the same as	too much	what have you

- You see someone you knew when you were 10 years old.
  Hey, [1] ______________ a long time! How [2] ______________ ?
- You run into an old classmate.
  Wow, I [3] ______________ since last semester! [4] ______________ been up to?
- An old teacher asks you what you've been doing since last year.
  Oh, not [5] ______________ . Just [6] ______________ usual.

B **Complete the conversation with expressions for catching up with people's news or comments with *that would be*.**

A Hi, it's so great to see you. [1] ______________ .
B I know! [2] ______________ since last spring when we had that class together.
A I can't believe we ran into each other here. [3] ______________ ?
B [4] ______________ . I'm still going to school, and I've been working full-time since July. [5] ______________ ?
A Oh, [6] ______________ . I've been taking classes full-time. Hey, are you busy right now? Do you want to get some dinner?
B [7] ______________ . Where should we go?
A Well, I've been thinking about Chinese food all day because someone in my office was eating some.
B Oh, I know a fantastic Chinese restaurant. You don't order your food. The servers just bring you whatever the chef is cooking.
A [8] ______________ .
B Great! Let's go!

8.4 A TIME-SAVING TIP

1 LISTENING

A 8.01 LISTEN FOR MAIN AND SUPPORTING IDEAS **Listen to the podcast. Answer the questions.**

1 What is the first tip? ______
2 What is an example of the first tip? ______
3 How is the first tip helpful for Tina? ______
4 What is the second tip? ______
5 How is the second tip helpful for Tina? ______
6 According to Andrew, which of the two tips can save you more time? ______

2 READING

A **Read the comment by BusyBee221. Then read the statements and check (✓) the ones that are true.**

BusyBee221 wrote:

After I listened to the latest episode of *Tips with Tina*, I immediately decided to try Andrew's tips for saving time. Like Tina, I'm always losing my keys. I also spend a lot of time looking for my wallet in the morning. So, I put a bowl on the dresser in my bedroom, and I started putting my keys and my wallet in it when I got home every evening. I tried it for a week, and it really made a difference. Before, I used to feel rushed every morning, and I would sometimes get to class late, but now I don't feel rushed at all. I got to class on time every day last week, and I even had time to stop for coffee on my way to school.

The second tip was harder to follow, but I did my best. I managed to say "no" to one invitation last week when my friend invited me to a movie. I felt guilty about it for a while, but I was really glad that I refused the invitation. While my friend was at the movies, I finished my paper for my history class. It felt great!

So far, Andrew's tips are working for me. I think they'll keep saving me time in the future.

reply

☐ 1 BusyBee221 tried Andrew's tips.
☐ 2 He started putting his wallet and keys in a bowl by the front door.
☐ 3 He didn't have to look for his keys, but he still got to class late every morning.
☐ 4 He said "no" to one friend's invitation.
☐ 5 He was able to write a paper because he didn't go to the movies with his friend.
☐ 6 He wishes that he had said "yes" to his friend.

3 WRITING

A **Write your own comment responding to Tina's podcast and BusyBee221's comment. Decide if you think Andrew's tips are helpful.**

CHECK AND REVIEW

Read the statements. Can you do these things?

UNIT 8	Mark the boxes. ☑ I can do it. ? I am not sure. **I can …**	If you are not sure, go back to these pages in the Student's Book.
VOCABULARY	☐ **describe experiences.** ☐ **describe progress.**	page 76 page 78
GRAMMAR	☐ **use the present perfect continuous.** ☐ **use the present perfect and the present perfect continuous.**	page 77 page 79
FUNCTIONAL LANGUAGE	☐ **ask about someone's news and say how long it's been.** ☐ **use *that would be* to comment on something.**	page 80 page 81
SKILLS	☐ **write a post about managing your time.** ☐ **use time expressions.**	page 83 page 83

UNIT 9 MAKE IT WORK

9.1 BUILDING A FUTURE

1 VOCABULARY: College subjects

A **Match each subject with a possible job description.**

1 architecture ___h___
2 biology ______
3 business ______
4 chemistry ______
5 computer science ______
6 economics ______
7 education ______
8 engineering ______
9 law ______
10 medicine ______
11 physics ______
12 political science ______

a build machines and bridges
b study the way people use money
c study chemical reactions
d work in government
e start your own company
f take care of sick people
g study how light and energy work
h design buildings
i understand the rules of society
j create websites
k study living things
l help people learn

2 GRAMMAR: Modals of necessity: *have to, need to, must*

A **Circle the correct words to complete the sentences.**

1 I *must* / *didn't have to* take chemistry because I wasn't a chemistry major.
2 I *has to* / *have to* take political science this semester.
3 She *doesn't need to* / *don't need to* take any political science classes.
4 We *needs to* / *need to* sign up for classes today.
5 All students *has to* / *must* choose a major by the spring.
6 I think I want to major in architecture, but I'm not sure. I *need* / *need to* take some classes and see how it goes before I decide.

B **Find the mistakes and write correct questions. Then answer with true information.**

1 Did you had to take the class twice?

Did you have to take the class twice?

No, I didn't have to take it twice. I only had to take it once.

2 Do the rules say that you must to get to class on time?

3 Do I need to taking a business class to get a good job?

4 Is it true that students don't must choose majors at the beginning of the term?

5 Does the teacher has to give a final exam?

6 Do we have to going to class next Monday?

3 GRAMMAR AND VOCABULARY

A **Write answers to the questions. Use *have to*, *don't have to*, and *must* in your answers.**

1 If you want to work in city government, what kinds of classes do you have to take?

2 Do you know someone who is a science major? What are some of the courses that they don't need to take?

3 Henry wants to design houses. What kinds of classes does he need to take?

4 Alice is taking business classes. What do you think her career goal is?

5 What is your career goal? What kinds of classes do you need to take to succeed in that career?

9.2 HOUSE RULES

1 VOCABULARY: Employment

A **Unscramble the letters to make words.**

1	eemloyrp	*employer*	7	lyapp	
2	gmnaae		8	ccattonr	
3	eiofoprssn		9	eeettirrmn	
4	aeerrc		10	eihr	
5	wigknor orhsu		11	refi	
6	aweg		12	lsryaa	

B **Complete the email with the correct form of the words from exercise 1A. The first letter of each word is given to you.**

To: All students
From: President Galarza
Subject: New Work-Readiness Course

The university is now offering a work-readiness course to help any student who is about to graduate and start a new [1] *career* . The course is designed to prepare you for any [2]p ________ – from architect to accountant. Topics cover how to [3]a ________ for a new position, how to make sure you get a fair [4]s ________ or [5]w ________, and how to successfully [6]m ________ other workers. This course will teach you how to succeed as an employee from the moment you are [7]h ________ until [8]r ________. Instructors will answer questions about different kinds of [9]e ________ and can offer advice before you sign a [10]c ________. Please visit the university's homepage to sign up.

2 GRAMMAR: Modals of prohibition and permission

A **Put the words in the correct places in the chart. You will use one word twice.**

can can't could may may not must not

It is not allowed.	You have permission.	You don't have permission.

B **Complete the sentences with the words in the box. Different answers are possible.**

can	can't	could	may	must not

1 This is the third time you've been late. You can't / must not be late for work again.

2 ________ I take a break now? I need to eat something.

3 You ________ work at home on Friday. I'd like you to be here in person for the meeting.

4 He ________ come to the meeting. He might have some good ideas to share.

5 ________ I work on the project, too? It sounds like fun.

3 GRAMMAR AND VOCABULARY

A **Think of someone you know who can work from home sometimes. Answer the questions.**

1 What is his or her job?

____

2 Who is his or her employer?

____

3 What is his or her salary or hourly wage? If you're not sure, you can guess.

____

4 How often can he or she work from home? Are there times when he or she *can't* work from home?

____

____

5 Does this person find it easy or difficult to manage his or her time? Explain.

____

____

6 What are his or her working hours from home? Can they be different from the hours at his or her usual workplace?

____

____

7 Would you like to have his or her job and the ability to work from home? Why or why not?

____

____

9.3 A NEW CHALLENGE

1 FUNCTIONAL LANGUAGE: Expressing confidence and lack of confidence

A **Match each statement with a response.**

1 That won't be a problem.	____	a Why not?
2 I'm not sure I can handle that.	____	b Great!
3 I don't think I'm strong enough.	____	c Oh, but it's really easy.
4 That doesn't bother me.	____	d I'm glad to hear that.
5 I think I can handle that.	____	e You'll be fine. Don't worry.
6 That concerns me a little.	____	f Then let's start tomorrow.

2 REAL-WORLD STRATEGY: Focusing on reasons

A **Insert the phrase *The thing is* in the correct place in each sentence.**

The thing is,

1 Basketball? I'm not sure I can handle that. ^ I can't throw very well.

2 Thanks for inviting me, but I can't go. I have to study for a test.

3 I'd love to go, but I have to stay home tonight. I have to take care of my roommate because she's sick.

4 I don't think I'm strong enough. I broke my leg a few months ago. I was skiing with some friends.

5 I don't think I can make it. But thanks for asking. I had to work late last night, and I'm really tired.

3 FUNCTIONAL LANGUAGE AND REAL-WORLD STRATEGY

A **Complete each conversation with a phrase in the box and *The thing is*.**

I don't think I'm strong enough.
I'm not sure I can handle that.
That concerns me a little.

Conversation 1

A Would you like to go skateboarding with me and some of my friends on Saturday?

B No thanks. 1 ___The thing is___, I've never skateboarded before.

A It's easy! And it's fun. We usually skate down that big hill by the park.

B That sounds really scary! 2 ______________________

A Oh, I think you can. You should at least try it once.

Conversation 2

A Do you want to go to a yoga class with me?

B 3 ______________________

A You don't have to be. It mostly involves stretching.

B Thanks for asking, but I don't think so. 4 ______________________, I don't think I'll like it.

Conversation 3

A How long is this hike going to be?

B It's not a long hike – just a couple of miles. And it ends at the top of a mountain! It's beautiful.

A 5 ______________________, but I guess it will be OK.

B What are you worried about?

A I'm worried about going to the top of the mountain. 6 ______________________, I'm kind of afraid of heights.

9.4 A JOB SEARCH

1 READING

A **Read the job ad for a computer programmer and the two résumés. Then choose the best person for the job.**

The best person for the job is ______________________ .

Responsibilities:
You will help us create computer programs and applications. You will also write reviews of other companies' programs and apps. You can make your own working hours, but you must come into the office in downtown Los Angeles once a week.

Qualifications:
You need to have a four-year degree in computer science. You should have at least two years of work experience. You must have good communication and writing skills and work well with a team.

Katya Petrov

345 Fell Street, Dallas, Texas 75001 415-555-9921 kpetrov77@cup.org

PROFESSIONAL PROFILE

I have a degree in computer science with five years of experience as a computer programmer at an online startup. I wrote articles about technology for my college newspaper, where I worked closely with a group of writers, editors, and photographers.

Elisa Gómez García

1733 J Street, Los Angeles, California 90015 310-555-2910 egomezgarcia@cup.org

PROFESSIONAL PROFILE

I have a degree in computer science with two years of experience creating smartphone apps for a large international company. While I was in college, I was the manager of the computer lab. I worked with a team of five, and I wrote a newsletter for the computer science department.

B READ FOR DETAIL **Identify the information in the profile of the best candidate that makes her the right person for the job.**

1 degree: ______________________
2 experience: ______________________
3 writing skills: ______________________
4 teamwork: ______________________
5 location: ______________________

2 LISTENING

A 9.01 **Listen to Min-kyu talking to Laura about his work experience. Then read the statements and check (✓) *True, False,* or *Not given*. Then listen again and correct the false statements.**

	True	False	Not given
1 Min-kyu has a degree in business.	☐	☑	☐
He has a degree in law.			
2 He was an office assistant in a law office.	☐	☐	☐
3 He organizes schedules in his current job.	☐	☐	☐
4 He wrote computer programs.	☐	☐	☐
5 He studied Korean in college.	☐	☐	☐

3 WRITING

A **Think of someone you know who has an interesting or unusual job. Imagine what information is on that person's résumé. Complete the résumé with information about that person. Use parallel structures in your bulleted lists.**

CONTACT INFORMATION ______

EXPERIENCE
- ______
- ______
- ______
- ______
- ______

SKILLS
- ______
- ______

EDUCATION
- ______
- ______

CHECK AND REVIEW

Read the statements. Can you do these things?

UNIT 9	Mark the boxes. ☑ I can do it. ? I am not sure. **I can …**	If you are not sure, go back to these pages in the Student's Book.
VOCABULARY	☐ **talk about college subjects.** ☐ **talk about employment.**	page 86 page 88
GRAMMAR	☐ **use modals of necessity: *have to, need to, must.*** ☐ **use modals of prohibition and permission.**	page 87 page 89
FUNCTIONAL LANGUAGE	☐ **express confidence or lack of confidence.** ☐ **use *the thing is* to focus on reasons.**	page 90 page 91
SKILLS	☐ **write the main part of a résumé.** ☐ **use parallel structures.**	page 93 page 93

UNIT 10 WHY WE BUY

10.1 GREEN CLOTHES

1 VOCABULARY: Describing materials

A **Check (✓) all of the adjectives that describe each item.**

	Hard	Soft	Natural	Artificial
1 cotton T-shirt	☐	☑	☑	☐
2 glass vase	☐	☐	☐	☐
3 leather wallet	☐	☐	☐	☐
4 metal key	☐	☐	☐	☐
5 plastic bag	☐	☐	☐	☐
6 polyester pants	☐	☐	☐	☐
7 stone wall	☐	☐	☐	☐
8 wood house	☐	☐	☐	☐
9 wool sweater	☐	☐	☐	☐

B **Write two objects that match each description. For each item, choose one object from the box and add one of your own ideas.**

a big box of books	a bookshelf	a pair of thick socks
a pencil	a raincoat	~~a water glass~~

1 fragile: a water glass ________________

2 heavy: ________________ ________________

3 light: ________________ ________________

4 strong: ________________ ________________

5 warm: ________________ ________________

6 waterproof: ________________ ________________

2 GRAMMAR: Simple present passive

A **Check (✓) the passive sentences. Circle the passive verbs.**

☑ **1** This shirt (is made) of eco-friendly organic cotton.

☐ **2** That color looks great on you.

☐ **3** Does this hat look silly on me?

☐ **4** Jeans are worn by people all over the world.

☐ **5** In most places, shorts aren't sold in the winter.

☐ **6** How many pairs of shoes are sold every day?

B **Complete the sentences with the simple present passive forms of the verbs in the box.**

~~give~~ make sell use wear write

1 Every time someone buys a pair of shoes, another pair *is given* to someone who needs them.
2 Who ________ this book ________ by? I can't read the author's name.
3 Plastic ________ in millions of different products, from water bottles to cars.
4 ________ winter coats ________ here?
5 What ________ this sweater ________ of?
6 These days, jeans ________ to formal and informal events.

3 GRAMMAR AND VOCABULARY

A **Make sentences with the phrases and verbs in the chart. Add two of your own ideas. Use the simple present passive forms of the verbs.**

Waterproof materials	make	in the earth
This T-shirt	use	easily
Most boots	break	of cotton
Metal	need	in the winter
Fragile objects	find	in rain boots
A warm coat		of leather
________		________
________		________

1 *Waterproof materials are used in rain boots.*
2 ________
3 ________
4 ________
5 ________
6 ________
7 ________
8 ________

10.2 GLOBAL OR LOCAL?

1 VOCABULARY: Production and distribution

A **Find 12 more vocabulary words in the word search.**

catch	~~deliver~~	design	export	freeze
grow	import	manufacture	pick	produce
ship	store	transport		

D	E	R	T	C	I	S	H	E	N	I	L	O	I	I	R	V
E	D	X	R	X	R	E	W	Y	K	G	W	A	H	M	E	D
X	E	Y	A	U	S	R	W	O	H	P	F	M	U	P	O	C
P	L	O	N	N	P	R	O	D	U	C	E	M	L	O	T	B
A	I	M	S	F	H	A	E	K	R	S	C	J	U	R	I	P
C	V	E	P	A	K	E	X	P	O	R	T	R	I	T	N	L
R	E	A	O	B	X	Y	P	L	W	A	R	G	P	I	C	K
S	R	E	R	A	N	U	G	C	W	Q	P	X	U	C	M	O
T	E	R	T	W	O	L	G	K	S	H	I	P	O	A	S	U
B	S	P	E	X	P	O	R	T	S	T	Y	P	W	T	E	R
C	A	Y	C	R	J	I	O	D	E	U	L	N	M	C	O	Z
Z	R	F	U	N	W	O	W	P	M	C	F	T	S	H	G	P
F	R	H	Z	W	A	O	L	E	F	T	R	Y	N	I	W	Z
G	M	A	N	U	F	A	C	T	U	R	E	T	R	I	V	S
E	X	O	L	P	W	D	T	B	W	C	E	N	O	W	X	R
C	S	T	O	R	E	S	L	O	P	E	Z	R	T	U	B	C
M	E	S	A	Y	W	J	W	E	I	D	E	S	I	G	N	L

2 GRAMMAR: Simple past passive

A **Find the mistakes and write correct sentences.**

1 These flowers was cut yesterday.

These flowers were cut yesterday.

2 The oranges were take to grocery stores.

3 All of the milk were produced in the local area.

4 The coffee was ship from Guatemala.

5 Most of our vegetables grown in California.

6 These herbs was planted last year.

B **Use the words to write sentences or questions in the simple past passive.**

1 these vegetables / grow / on nearby farms / ?

Were these vegetables grown on nearby farms?

2 the rice / not produce / here / .

3 the fruit / import / from South America / .

4 all of the food / make / by local restaurants / .

5 where / these plates / produce / ?

3 GRAMMAR AND VOCABULARY

A **Circle the best verb for each sentence. Then complete each sentence with the simple past passive form of the verb.**

1 Too many fish *were caught* last year, so fishing is not allowed this year.
   a manufacture **b** grow **(c)** catch

2 This meat ________, and sometimes the cold temperature changes the taste.
   a export **b** pick **c** freeze

3 Where ________ your cell phone ________? In China?
   a manufacture **b** import **c** grow

4 The package ________ yesterday. Did you receive it?
   a export **b** deliver **c** produce

5 These strawberries are really fresh. They ________ this morning.
   a pick **b** freeze **c** design

10.3 WHAT TO BUY?

1 FUNCTIONAL LANGUAGE: Questioning and approving of someone's choices

A **Circle the best expressions to complete the conversations.**

Conversation 1

A I'm going to order the pizza.

B [1]*Do you really need that? / Are you sure you want to get that?* Cheese always gives you a stomachache.

A That's true. OK, I'll get the salmon.

B [2]*Why would you want to buy that? / I think you made the right choice.* I'll get the salmon, too!

Conversation 2

A I'm going to buy this Bluetooth speaker.

B [3]*Why would you want to buy that? / Now that's a good idea.* It doesn't sound very good.

A I know, but it's shaped like a little bear. It's funny.

B [4]*Do you really need a bad speaker? / I think you made the right choice.*

A No, I guess not. I'll put it back.

B [5]*Are you sure you want to get that? / That's what I would do.*

2 REAL-WORLD STRATEGY: Changing your mind

A **In each conversation, write the bold expression in the correct place. Write an ✘ where the expression can't go.**

1 **On second thought,**

A I'm going to buy a chicken to cook for dinner.

B That sounds good. ______________ How are you going to cook it?

A Maybe I'll roast it. ______________ I'm going to make spaghetti. ______________ We had chicken last night.

B I love spaghetti. ______________ Can I come over for dinner?

A Sure!

2 **Now that I think about it,**

A This looks like a fun game. I'm going to get it.

B I think I played that game at Sam's house.

A Oh, really? ______________ I thought it was new.

B ______________ It's been out for about a month.

A Oh. ______________ I already have it at home! ______________ I forgot I had it.

3 FUNCTIONAL LANGUAGE AND REAL-WORLD STRATEGY

A **Complete the conversation with the phrases in the box.**

On second thought	Now that's a good idea.	Why would you want to buy a new one?

A I'm going to buy a new tablet this weekend.

B Don't you already have one?

A Well, I used to have one, but I gave it to my sister.

B That's very generous! Why did you give it to her?

A Because she needed one. And anyway, I didn't really use mine.

B [1] ____________________ You never used your old one!

A That's true. [2] ____________________ , maybe I'll save my money.

B [3] ____________________

B **Read the situation about two people. Write a conversation like the one in exercise 3A. Use the phrases in the box.**

Person A wants to buy a jacket. It's too small, but it's on sale.

Person B tries to convince Person A not to buy the jacket.

I think you made the right choice.	Are you sure you want to get that?
Now that I think about it	

A ____________________

B ____________________

A ____________________

B ____________________

A ____________________

B ____________________

A ____________________

B ____________________

10.4 NOT JUST CUSTOMERS – FANS

1 LISTENING

A 10.01 LISTEN FOR DETAIL **Listen to the podcast. Answer the questions.**

1 What kind of company do Jackie and Christopher have?

It's a cookie company.

2 When did they close their company?

____

3 Why did they start their business again?

____

4 How is the business different now?

____

5 Where are their customers?

____

2 READING

A **Read a customer's feedback about Cookie Bites. Answer the questions.**

Shop Reviews Account Basket

I ordered four boxes of your Cookie Bites last week because a friend of mine recommended them to me. They were delivered yesterday, and they're almost all gone! My roommates and I loved them. I had to hide one box in my room so they wouldn't be eaten by my hungry roommates. I bought four different flavors: chocolate chip, peanut butter, double chocolate, and coconut. The chocolate chip and peanut butter were my favorite kinds. Although I love chocolate, the double chocolate ones were a little too rich and sweet for me. I'm sure the coconut cookies were delicious. However, I never got to try one because my roommates ate them all. I'm so excited to try the rest of the flavors!

EDISON

1 What product is Edison's feedback about?

It's about Cookie Bites.

2 What is his general opinion about the product?

____

3 Is his feedback all positive, all negative, or a little of both? Explain.

____

4 Who did he share the product with?

____

5 Is he going to buy the product again? How do you know?

____

3 WRITING

A **Think of a product that you use every day and don't really think about, such as toothpaste, dish soap, or shampoo.**

- What is the product?
- Why do you continue to buy the same product?
- What do you like about it?
- What do you dislike about it?

B **Write a post giving feedback about the product from exercise 3A. Use *however* and *although* to contrast ideas.**

CHECK AND REVIEW

Read the statements. Can you do these things?

UNIT 10	Mark the boxes. ☑ I can do it. ? I am not sure. **I can …**	If you are not sure, go back to these pages in the Student's Book.
VOCABULARY	☐ **describe materials.** ☐ **talk about production and distribution.**	page 98 page 100
GRAMMAR	☐ **use the simple present form of the passive.** ☐ **use the simple past form of the passive.**	page 99 page 101
FUNCTIONAL LANGUAGE	☐ **question or approve of someone's choices.** ☐ **use expressions for changing your mind.**	page 102 page 103
SKILLS	☐ **write feedback about company products.** ☐ **use *however* and *although* to contrast ideas.**	page 105 page 105

UNIT 11 PUSHING YOURSELF

11.1 SECRETS OF SUCCESS

1 VOCABULARY: Succeeding

A **Complete the sentences with the words in the box and the correct prepositions (*at*, *out*, *over*, or *up*).**

figure get ~~give~~ give keep set stand work work

1 My economics class is really hard, but I don't want to ___give up___ yet. I know I can do better.
2 If you ________________ writing well, you'll get better at it.
3 You're doing a great job. ________________ the good work.
4 I don't stay mad. I ________________ things quickly.
5 I ________________. Learning how to code is too hard. I can't do it.
6 My laptop isn't working, and I can't ________________ what's wrong.
7 I want to ________________ my own business as soon as I graduate from college.
8 This job opportunity didn't ________________, but don't worry. You have three more interviews this month.
9 People ________________ at work when they work hard to achieve big goals. Colleagues notice them.

2 GRAMMAR: Phrasal verbs

A **Put each phrasal verb from exercise 1A in the correct place in the chart.**

No object	With object, separable	With object, inseparable
	give up	

B **Use phrasal verbs in the chart to complete the sentences so they are true for you.**

1 I always try my hardest to speak English with my teacher. Even though it is difficult sometimes, I never ___give up___ .
2 I think I've been doing a really good job ________________ lately. I hope to ________________ it ________________ and continue my success.
3 ________________ is someone who I think is always the most interesting person in the room. This person almost always ________________ in a crowd.
4 I was having trouble finding the answer to a problem in my life recently, but I finally ________________ it ________________. Now I know I have to ________________ .

3 GRAMMAR AND VOCABULARY

A **Find the errors in the phrasal verbs. Write correct sentences.**

1 If you don't want to stand it out in a group, don't ask a lot of questions.
If you don't want to stand out in a group, don't ask a lot of questions.

2 I'm going to set my office out today.

3 Your work has been excellent. Keep up it.

4 I'm working out being a better listener because I want to be a good manager.

5 When you fail, it can be hard to get it over.

6 Can you help me figure out it?

7 Don't give it up! You can do it!

B **Answers the questions.**

1 When you work at something for a while and it doesn't work out, what do you do?

2 Have you ever given up and quit a job, a class, a club, or something else? What was it? Why did you give up?

3 How do you get over big disappointments?

4 Do you like to stand out? Why or why not?

11.2 NOW THAT'S INTERESTING!

1 VOCABULARY: Opportunities and risks

A **Circle the correct words to complete the sentences.**

1 Can I borrow your laptop? I need to do some *research* / *options*.
2 You should carefully *reward* / *consider* your decision before you decide whether to quit your job.
3 One of my *goals* / *situations* is to go to college.
4 The *purpose* / *situation* of this visit is to see if I like the city enough to move there.
5 There are *risks and goals* / *advantages and disadvantages* to working part-time. One good thing is you have more time for school and family. One bad thing is you don't make as much money as you would with a full-time job.
6 I have a couple of *effects* / *options*. I can work and save money for a couple of years and then go to school, or I can take out a loan and go to school now.
7 I applied for 30 jobs last month. The *risk* / *result* was that I got five job offers!
8 I found someone's wallet on the street and sent it to him in the mail. He offered me a $100 *reward* / *result*!
9 Quitting my job is a big *risk* / *effect* because it's hard to find a job right now, but I'm really unhappy at work.
10 I can't get a job without a driver's license, but I can't get a driver's license until I have an address here. And I can't pay for a new apartment without a job. It's a strange *purpose* / *situation*.
11 Traveling to other countries has had a really positive *goal* / *effect* on my life. It has given me a lot of self-confidence.

2 GRAMMAR: Present and future unreal conditionals

A **Match the sentence halves.**

1 If it were nice outside,	d	a	if her company allowed it.
2 If I had to choose a place to go for dinner,	____	b	if you met her.
3 You would like my friend Sarah	____	c	I would visit my sister more often.
4 I would be happier with my job	____	d	I wouldn't have to wear this big coat.
5 If I had a car,	____	e	he would study architecture.
6 Michael would start his own business	____	f	they would buy a condo by the beach.
7 Cynthia would join the gym nearby	____	g	if he had more startup money.
8 If David went back to school,	____	h	I would pick a Vietnamese restaurant.
9 If Vince and Mary sold their house,	____	i	if the membership weren't so expensive.
10 Michelle would work from home	____	j	if it weren't so far away.

B Complete each sentence with the correct forms of the verbs in parentheses ( ). Then answer the questions so they are true for you.

1 A If I ___owned___ (own) a big house, I ________ (ask) my family to live with me. Would you?
  B No, but I think I'd ask all my friends to live with me if I owned a big house!
2 A I ________ (not quit) my job if I ________ (have) a million dollars. What about you?
  B ________
3 A If my friends ________ (move) far away, I ________ (be) sad. How would you feel?
  B ________
4 A If your best friend ________ (not work) with you, who ________ you ________ (talk to) all day?
  B ________
5 A ________ the people you live with ________ (be) happy if you ________ (buy) a huge new TV?
  B ________
6 A Where ________ you ________ (live) if you ________ (have) the chance to live anywhere?
  B ________
7 A If you ________ (win) a free trip to a beautiful island, who ________ you ________ (take) with you?
  B ________

3 GRAMMAR AND VOCABULARY

A **Complete the sentences with your own ideas.**

1 I would consider moving to a new town or city if ________.
2 I wouldn't mind risking my job if ________.
3 If I were in a scary situation in a strange city, ________.
4 I would have more advantages if ________.
5 If I knew that I would definitely get a good result, ________.

11.3 IT'S NOT WORTH IT

1 FUNCTIONAL LANGUAGE: Asking for agreement and agreeing

A **Complete the conversations with the words in the box.**

agree	~~don't~~	especially	know	mean	point	right

A I've worked for this company for five years, and I've never gotten a raise. I should have gotten one by now, [1] ___don't___ you think?

B Yeah, [2] ________ when the company is doing so well.

A That's true. This has been the best five years in the history of the company, [3] ________ ?

B Yes, you're right.

A Everyone who has been here during that time should get a raise, you [4] ________ ?

B Yeah, I would [5] ________ with you. I think we've all helped the company grow over the last five years.

A And our team even came up with *all* of the new product ideas in the last three years.

B Good [6] ________ . We should all ask Lúcio for a raise!

A We should! But I don't think we should do it today.

B Why not?

A Lúcio is in a really bad mood today, and when he's in a bad mood, he says "no" to everything.

B I see what you [7] ________ . Let's do it when he's in a better mood.

2 REAL-WORLD STRATEGY: Softening an opinion

A **Rewrite the opinions. Use *I guess* or *I feel like* to soften them. More than one answer is possible.**

1 The TV is so loud. We should ask him to turn it down.

The TV is so loud. I guess we should ask him to turn it down.

2 I don't see the house. We're going the wrong way.

____

3 It's too late to call Dan. Let's call him tomorrow.

____

4 We've been waiting for a long time. The bus isn't going to come.

____

5 This cake tastes terrible. They used salt instead of sugar.

____

B **Match the scenarios with the opinions.**

1 The movie has started, but Claudio hasn't arrived. ____
2 You went to the address of the florist you used last year, but there's a shoe store there now. ____
3 You had a job interview and you couldn't answer a lot of the questions. ____
4 You were going to fly home today, but you broke your leg, so you have to stay a couple more days. ____
5 Sandra is very unhappy at work, and she complains about it a lot. ____

a "I guess the store went out of business."
b "I feel like she should quit her job."
c "I guess he got stuck in traffic."
d "I guess I have to change my flight."
e "I feel like I'm not going to get the job."

3 FUNCTIONAL LANGUAGE AND REAL-WORLD STRATEGY

A **Complete the conversation using the expressions in the box. Use at least two expressions from each column.**

Don't you think?	Yeah, especially when	I guess
, right?	Yeah, I would agree with you.	I feel like
Don't you agree?	Good point.	
, you know?	I see what you mean.	

A I'm trying to choose between two jobs. One of them is for a law office. It pays really well, but there's no chance for promotion. The other is for an online magazine. It doesn't pay as much, but I could get a promotion and more money eventually.

B *You don't really need a lot of money right now because you're living with your parents. Don't you think?*

A ____

B ____

A ____

B ____

A ____

11.4 OUTSIDE THE COMFORT ZONE

1 READING

A **READ FOR DETAIL** **Read the article. Then answer the questions.**

The Helper Experiment

by Thomas Holley

I recently heard that helping others is a good way to achieve happiness. I wondered if this could be true, so I decided to try it. I came up with an experiment: for one month, I would do at least one nice thing for another person every day. This could be anything from holding a door open to taking care of a sick friend.

On the first day, I saw my elderly neighbor carrying a heavy trash bag to the trash can outside. She was really struggling. I went up to her and asked if I could help her. She gratefully gave me the bag, and we started walking back toward our apartment building. When we got to the front door, she thanked me and invited me into her apartment for a cup of tea. We chatted over our tea for a while, and then I went home. I have to say, I felt great! I felt like I did something important that day and made my neighbor's life a little easier.

Over the next few days, I found myself doing more than one nice thing per day. On my day off the first week, I spent almost the whole day looking for people to help. I wanted to figure out exactly why helping people was making me happy, so I did some research. I found out that there are a number of ways that helping people affects us. For example, helping people can increase our self-esteem and confidence. Doing something nice for another person can also give us a sense of purpose. In addition, when we volunteer on a regular basis, we feel a sense of belonging to a group.

During that month, I think I probably did at least a hundred nice things for others. Since then, I've kept up doing at least one helpful thing per day. If I didn't have to work, I would help people all day long! I've even started volunteering at the hospital. I think everyone should try this experiment. It can make us all happier.

1 What point of view does the writer use? *first person*

2 Why did the writer decide to try the "helper experiment"? ______________________

____

3 Who did the writer help first? ______________________

4 How did the writer feel after the first day of the experiment? ______________________

____

5 What are three reasons that helping people makes us happy? ______________________

____

2 LISTENING

A 11.01 **Listen to the podcast. Complete the sentences.**

1 The speakers are both ______________________ .

2 Helping others can have ______________________ on our brains.

3 It can produce chemicals that ______________________ .

4 These chemicals make us want to ______________________ .

5 Helping people can reduce ______________________ .

3 WRITING

A **Write a personal story about a time when you helped someone, or write a story about a time when someone helped you. Explain what happened and how it made you feel.**

CHECK AND REVIEW

Read the statements. Can you do these things?

UNIT 11	Mark the boxes. ☑ I can do it. ? I am not sure. **I can …**	If you are not sure, go back to these pages in the Student's Book.
VOCABULARY	☐ **talk about succeeding.** ☐ **talk about opportunities and risks.**	page 108 page 110
GRAMMAR	☐ **use phrasal verbs.** ☐ **use future unreal conditionals.**	page 109 page 111
FUNCTIONAL LANGUAGE	☐ **ask for agreement and agree.** ☐ **soften an opinion.**	page 112 page 113
SKILLS	☐ **write a personal story.** ☐ **use *On the one hand* and *On the other hand* to compare opposite ways of thinking.**	page 115 page 115

UNIT 12 LIFE'S LITTLE LESSONS

12.1 IT WAS AN ACCIDENT!

1 VOCABULARY: Describing accidents

A **Match the words with their definitions.**

1 be mad at	g	a not to turn something off
2 blame	____	b to feel sorry for something you did
3 damage	____	c to accidently hit something and make it fall
4 destroy	____	d to cause some harm, like scratches or dents
5 fall out	____	e not to close something
6 feel bad (about)	____	f to accidentally drop liquid
7 knock off	____	g to feel angry with
8 leave on	____	h to take something out of somewhere
9 leave open	____	i to think something is someone's fault
10 pick up	____	j to move something around quickly
11 pull out	____	k to break so badly that repair is impossible
12 shake	____	l to lift something with your hands
13 slip	____	m to suddenly move out of the correct position or place
14 spill	____	n to drop out of somewhere

B **Circle the correct answers to complete the conversation**

A Who 1*spilled / dropped* water on the floor?

B Sorry, Mom. It was me. I accidentally 2*fell / knocked* a glass 3*off / out* of the table.

A That's OK. I'm not 4*mad / feel bad* at you. Let's clean the water off the floor. I don't want anyone to 5*slip / fall out*.

B Oh, there's broken glass on the floor, too. I'll 6*pick / pull* it 7*out / up*.

2 GRAMMAR: Indefinite pronouns

A **Complete the sentences with the words in parentheses ( ).**

1 (something, somewhere, someone)
I think ________________ spilled ________________ in the kitchen. It smells funny ________________ near the refrigerator.

2 (everywhere, everyone, everything)
________________ is broken because ________________ is throwing things ________________!

3 (anyone, anywhere, anything)
I can't find ________________ to read ________________. Does ________________ have a book I can borrow?

4 (nothing, no one, nowhere)
There's ________________ on the stove. I guess ________________ cooked dinner, but there's ________________ to get good food around here.

B **Complete the conversation with indefinite pronouns.**

A I'm trying to plan Mark's birthday party. I don't know [1] ___*anyone*___ who can cook. Do you?

B Yeah, I know [2] ______________ who cooks really well. Actually, you know him, too. It's Tómas. He's coming to the party.

A Oh, great. I didn't know he could cook.

B Yeah, he's really good. I have his email address around here [3] ______________. I'll need to tell him how much food to make. Do you know how many people are coming to the party?

A No, [4] ______________ has replied to the invitation yet. I guess [5] ______________ is busy studying for finals this week.

B That's too bad. I'll ask Tómas if he'll help us cook anyway. Is there [6] ______________ else I can do right now?

A No, there's really [7] ______________ else we can do until we know how many people are coming.

3 GRAMMAR AND VOCABULARY

A **Answer the questions.**

1 What do you usually do when you're mad at someone?

____

____

2 What would you do if you destroyed something in a friend's home?

____

____

3 Have you ever felt bad about anything? Explain.

____

____

4 What would you do if someone blamed you for something, but you didn't do anything wrong?

____

____

5 Imagine this: You're cooking dinner for friends. Some of the food falls on the kitchen floor after you've cooked it. No one sees this happen, but everyone knows that the food is ready. What would you do?

____

____

12.2 LEARNING UNDERWATER

1 VOCABULARY: Describing extremes

A **Write each word in the correct place in the chart.**

~~boiling~~	enormous	exhausted	freezing	huge	magnificent
miserable	starving	terrific	terrified	thrilled	tiny

Temperatures	Sizes	Emotions/Feelings	Opinions
boiling			

B **Complete the sentences with the correct words from exercise 1A.**

1 I'm ________________ that I got the job! I really wanted it!

2 Don't touch that water! I just turned off the heat and it's still ________________!

3 I have to give a presentation to 500 people tomorrow. I'm ________________!

4 This apartment is ________________. It's so much bigger than my apartment.

5 After work, I had to babysit my niece, and then I worked out at the gym for an hour. I'm ________________!

6 I'm always ________________ by about 11:00 a.m. I guess I should have a bigger breakfast.

7 We just met my friends' new kitten. She's so ________________ that she fits in my hand!

8 It's still snowing and our heater just broke. The house is ________________!

2 GRAMMAR: Reported speech

A **Match the direct speech with the reported speech.**

1 Mike: "I'm on a call with João." __b__

2 Anna: "I'm calling João." _____

3 Mike: "I'm going to call João." _____

4 Anna: "I was on a call with João." _____

5 Mike: "We can call João." _____

6 Anna: "I'll call João." _____

a Anna said she was calling João.

b Mike said he was on a call with João.

c Mike said they could call João.

d Anna said she had been on a call with João.

e Mike said he was going to call João.

f Anna said she would call João.

3 GRAMMAR AND VOCABULARY

A **Complete the conversation with the words in the box.**

exhausted freezing ~~miserable~~ starving terrific

Luna How was your hike on Saturday?

Terry It was [1] ___miserable___ ! I hated it.

Luna Oh no, why?

Terry It was [2] ______________ , and I didn't have a warm coat on.

Luna That doesn't sound like much fun.

Terry Well, I definitely won't do that hike again. How was your weekend?

Luna It was [3] ______________ . I saw a movie and went out to dinner with some friends.

Terry It sounds like you had a lot more fun than I did. I'm [4] ______________ . Do you want to go eat something somewhere?

Luna Sorry, I can't. It's late. I'm going to be [5] ______________ tomorrow if I don't go to bed soon.

B **Answer the questions with reported speech. Use the information from the conversation in exercise 3A.**

1 How was Terry's hike?
She said ______________________________ .

2 What was the weather like on the hike?
She said ______________________________ .

3 Is Terry going to do that hike again?
She said ______________________________ .

4 What did Luna do over the weekend?
She said ______________________________ .

5 Why does Terry want to get something to eat?
She said ______________________________ .

6 Why doesn't Luna want to get something to eat?
She said ______________________________ .

C **Read the situations. Use reported speech to tell what the people said to you. Add details.**

1 a time a friend was thrilled about some good news
My best friend Marina said she got a big promotion at work.

2 a time when a family member was miserable about some bad news
____

3 a time that someone you know felt terrified
____

4 a time when someone in your class or at your job was exhausted
____

12.3 A HOTEL NIGHTMARE

1 FUNCTIONAL LANGUAGE: Describing, asking about, and guessing feelings

A **Complete the words to make sentences. The first letter of each word is given to you.**

1 You must have been f_______________ .
2 What a n_______________ !
3 I bet that made you feel g_______________ .
4 Actually, I was s_______________ .
5 How did that make you f_______________ ?
6 I bet that made you feel b_______________ .

B **Complete the conversations with the sentences in exercise 1A.**

Conversation 1

A I thought you were going to be home yesterday.

B I was, but after I got to the airport, I found out that my flight was canceled! There wasn't another flight until the next day! [1] _______________

A [2] _______________ What did you do?

B I really was. I actually yelled at an airline employee. She told me that they had sent me a couple of emails about it.

A Did you get the emails?

B I remembered that I had gotten some emails from the airline, but I hadn't read them. So I read them and saw that she was right.

A [3] _______________

B Yeah, I felt awful.

Conversation 2

A How was your weekend at the beach?

B Well, Tom crashed the car into a tree right before we were going to leave.

A Oh no! [4] _______________

B Well, at first I felt mad, but it really wasn't Tom's fault. The brakes had stopped working, so he couldn't stop. Then the owners of the house we were renting felt bad for us, so they let us stay there for free while the car was being fixed.

A [5] _______________

B [6] _______________ We thought they didn't like us because they weren't very nice to us over the weekend. I'm glad we were wrong about that!

2 REAL-WORLD STRATEGY: Ending a story

A **Write endings to the stories to show they ended in a good way. Use *After all that* and *In the end*.**

Conversation 1

A I was really sick at the end of last year, and I missed my final exams.

B You must have been so upset!

A Actually, I was disappointed. I studied so hard all semester! But it's OK, ______________________

____

Conversation 2

A I didn't know my cell phone was in my pocket when I jumped into the pool yesterday.

B Oh no! Was it ruined? I bet you were so annoyed.

A Yeah, I was, at first. But ______________________

____

Conversation 3

A My train got stuck between stations when I was coming home last night.

B What a nightmare! Were you terrified?

A I was a little scared. ______________________

____

3 FUNCTIONAL LANGUAGE AND REAL-WORLD STRATEGY

A **Put the conversation in the correct order.**

Mari	I bet that made you feel good.	____
Mari	So what did you do?	____
Mari	You must have been furious!	____
Mari	Hey, didn't you go on a long road trip a few months ago?	1
Jack	I was lucky. I ran into an old friend. She loaned me some money.	____
Mari	How did that make you feel? Did you feel strange taking the money?	____
Jack	Yeah, I did. It was fun at first, but my money and credit cards were stolen.	____
Jack	No, I was so happy! To say thanks, I cooked dinner for her. We had so much fun.	____
Jack	It did. I couldn't stop smiling. In the end, we talked every day for three months, and now we're going to get married!	____
Jack	Actually, I was shocked because I'm always really careful. What a nightmare!	____

12.4 LESSONS LEARNED?

1 LISTENING

A 12.01 LISTEN FOR DETAIL **Listen to the lecture. Then complete the sentences.**

1 We can't change the past, but we can talk to people who have ______________________.
2 The speaker spoke with people who are ______________________.
3 She learned that important life lessons are ______________________.
4 Rose taught her that we need to take time to ______________________.
5 She said that we need friends who we can call ______________________.
6 Joe told her that people shouldn't ______________________.

2 READING

A **Read the anecdote. Answer the questions.**

When I was about 12 years old, I was mad at my best friend Andy because another boy told me that Andy had said mean things about me. I was so upset. Andy asked me what was wrong, but I wouldn't tell him. I wouldn't say anything. After a while, Andy was mad at me, too. We stopped talking to each other. I was miserable and I didn't know what to do. I wanted my best friend back, but I was still angry with him. After a couple of weeks, Andy and I both made new friends and we never talked to each other again.

That was a mistake that I won't make again. As I've gotten older, I've learned that it's important to tell your friends and family why you're mad. You might find out that there's actually no reason to be angry. Or you might discover that they had no idea that they had done something you didn't like. Years later, I found out that the other boy had lied to me. I felt bad that I had destroyed my friendship with my best friend just because I didn't tell him what was bothering me.

1 Why was the writer upset with Andy?

____

2 What did the writer do about his situation with Andy?

____

3 How did the situation affect his friendship with Andy?

____

4 What did the writer later learn about the other boy?

____

5 What life lesson did the writer learn from this situation?

____

3 WRITING

A **Think about a mistake you made in the past that you wouldn't make today. What lesson did you learn? Write an anecdote. Use different expressions to avoid repetition.**

CHECK AND REVIEW

Read the statements. Can you do these things?

UNIT 12	Mark the boxes. ☑ I can do it. ? I am not sure. **I can …**	If you are not sure, go back to these pages in the Student's Book.
VOCABULARY	☐ **describe accidents.** ☐ **describe extremes.**	page 118 page 120
GRAMMAR	☐ **use indefinite pronouns.** ☐ **use reported speech.**	page 119 page 121
FUNCTIONAL LANGUAGE	☐ **describe, ask about, and guess feelings.** ☐ **use *In the end* or *After all that* to end a story.**	page 122 page 123
SKILLS	☐ **write an anecdote about a life lesson.** ☐ **use different expressions to avoid repetition.**	page 125 page 125

7.5 TIME TO SPEAK Changing tastes

A **Think of a movie, TV show, or song that you liked five to ten years ago but don't like anymore.**

- Take notes on why you used to like it. Think of at least three reasons.
- Take notes on why you don't like it anymore. Think of at least three reasons.

B **Make a video of yourself describing your movie, TV show, or song. Explain why you used to like it and why you don't like it now. Share your videos in class. Did anyone have similar reasons why they used to like something? Did anyone have similar reasons why they don't like that thing now?**

8.5 TIME TO SPEAK Building a better life

A **Go online and research two time-saving tips that you haven't read about yet.**

- Take notes on the idea.
- Try each tip for a couple of days.
- Take notes on your experiences with the tips.

B **Make an audio recording. Record yourself explaining the tips and giving a review. Tell whether the tips worked or didn't work for you.**

9.5 TIME TO SPEAK Design your perfect job.

A **Go online and find an advertisement for a job that sounds fun to you.**

- Take notes on the qualifications and requirements. What kind of education and skills do you need to get this job?
- Write a résumé for a person who is qualified for the job.

B **Print out the job ad and present the ad and the résumé to the class. See if your classmates can think of other education or skills to add to the résumé.**

10.5 TIME TO SPEAK Shopping psychology

A **Think of a product people buy because they want to improve themselves or because they feel fear. Go online and find a picture or a commercial for the product.**

- Take notes about the product: What is it? How do people use it?
- How does the picture or commercial show what the product does to improve peoples' lives or make them feel safer? Take notes.

B **Show the picture or commercial for your product to your class. Describe what the product is. Explain how the picture or commercial convinces people to buy it. Do your classmates think the product can really improve peoples' lives or help them feel less fear?**

11.5 TIME TO SPEAK Success stories

A **Think of someone who became successful after appearing on a TV competition. You can find ideas on the Internet.**

- Take notes on the person's life before their success: Where did they live? What did they do? How were they trying to be successful? Why were they having trouble?
- Take notes on the TV competition. What kind of competition was it? What were the rules? What did the winner receive?
- Write a short summary of the person's life and how success changed it.

B **Present your summary to your class. If possible, show a short video clip of the person from their TV competition.**

12.5 TIME TO SPEAK Skillful fun

A **Think of something you had a difficult time learning when you were a child. For example, you might have had trouble figuring out how to tie your shoes, understanding the rules of soccer, or learning how to play an instrument.**

- Take notes on the situation: What were you learning? Why was it difficult? How did you feel about the situation?
- Take notes on how the situation ended: Did you keep trying or did you give up? Why? What did you learn?
- Make a video of yourself describing your experience.

B **Share your video with your class. Explain why you think this was or was not a valuable experience for you. If possible, demonstrate the skill to the class.**

NOTES

NOTES

The authors and publishers acknowledge the following sources of copyright material and are grateful for the permissions granted. While every effort has been made, it has not always been possible to identify the sources of all the material used, or to trace all copyright holders. If any omissions are brought to our notice, we will be happy to include the appropriate acknowledgements on reprinting and in the next update to the digital edition, as applicable.

Photographs
Key: B = Below, BR = Below Right, CL = Centre Left, CR = Centre Right, TR = Top Right.

All the photographs are sourced from Getty Images.

p. 50: Owen Franken/Corbis Documentary; p. 51: cristianl/E+; p. 52: demaerre/iStock/Getty Images Plus; p. 53: ThorMitty/iStock/Getty Images Plus; p. 57: Oliver Cleve/Photographer's Choice; p. 58: DragonImages/iStock/Getty Images Plus; p. 59: RoBeDeRo/E+; p. 60, p. 70: Blend Images – Jose Luis Pelaez Inc/Brand X Pictures; p. 61: kupicoo/E+; p. 63: DianaHirsch/iStock/Getty Images Plus; p. 65: White-Plaid/iStock/Getty Images Plus; p. 66: PeopleImages/DigitalVision; p. 67: ImagesBazaar; p 69 (TR): Mike Kemp/Blend Images; p. 69 (B): Ozgur Donmaz/Stockbyte; p. 74: dszc/E+; p. 75: Christina Esselman/Moment; p. 76: John S Lander/LightRocket; p. 77: Baloncici/iStock/Getty Images Plus; p. 79: gpointstudio/iStock/Getty Images Plus; p. 80: burwellphotography/E+; p. 84: Caiaimage/Rafal Rodzoch; p. 87: Lumina Images/Blend Images; p. 89: Piotr Marcinski/EyeEm; p. 91: fizkes/iStock/Getty Images Plus; p. 92: Jason Hosking/Taxi; p. 93: Amaia Arozena & Gotzon Iraola/Moment; p. 95: Martin Barraud/OJO Images; p. 96: Ben Gingell/iStock/Getty Images Plus.

Front cover photography by Alija/E+.

Illustration by Denis Cristo (Sylvie Poggio) p. 55.

Audio production by CityVox, New York.

Corpus
Development of this publication has made use of the Cambridge English Corpus (CEC). The CEC is a multi-billion word collection of contemporary spoken and written English. It includes British English, American English, and other varieties. It also includes the Cambridge Learner Corpus, the world's biggest collection of learner writing, developed in collaboration with Cambridge Assessment. Cambridge University Press uses the CEC to provide evidence about language use that helps to produce better language teaching materials.

Our Evolve authors study the Corpus to see how English is really used, and to identify typical learner mistakes. This information informs the authors' selection of vocabulary, grammar items and Student's Book Corpus features such as the Accuracy Check, Register Check, and Insider English.